A souvenir guide

575 Wandsworth Road

London

❀ National Trust

A Work of Art

575 Wandsworth Road sits quietly, set back from the bustle of the street on the south side of Wandsworth Road, a busy thoroughfare which connects Vauxhall and Clapham Junction in Lambeth, south London. This small, terraced house of 1819 is half-hidden by its front garden, and its unobtrusive exterior offers little hint of the rich and striking interior to be found inside.

The decoration was created by the Kenyan-born poet, novelist and civil servant, Khadambi Asalache (1935–2006), who bought the house in 1981, while working at the Treasury. Over a period of 19 years (from 1986) he turned his home into a work of art. Prompted by the need to disguise persistent damp in the basement dining room, he initially fixed floorboards to the damp wall. He went on to embellish almost every wall, ceiling and door in every room of the house with fretwork patterns and motifs, which he hand-carved from reclaimed pine doors and floorboards salvaged from skips. The house stands as he left it – filled with his handmade fretwork furniture and carefully arranged collections of beautiful and functional objects, including pressed-glass inkwells, pink and copper lustreware, postcards, woven wall hangings and books.

Khadambi Asalache left the house to the National Trust on his death in 2006 to ensure that it would be looked after and shared with a wider audience. Although he had decorated the house purely as a home for himself, he derived great pleasure from others' enjoyment of it and was convinced by the enthusiasm of his friends and acquaintances to seek the permanent preservation of his work. The National Trust acquired the house in 2010, recognising that it has national significance as both a home and a work of art.

Khadambi Asalache in the Dining Room in 1988. The pad saw Khadambi used to carve the fretwork and a section of partly carved pine are lent against the radiator. Photograph by Gered Mankowitz

The Rear Sitting Room

When Khadambi Asalache purchased the house in 1981, it was in a parlous state. A menagerie of animals, including a horse, a pig and chickens, had been kept in the back garden. Fortuitously, he was able to see beyond its outwardly worn appearance and was drawn to its elegant proportions, sunny garden and proximity to his office in Whitehall via the 77A bus.

By 1986, however, he was beset by damp in the basement dining room caused by the impermeable nature of the concrete floor of the adjoining commercial laundry. After several unsuccessful attempts by builders to cure the damp, he adopted what he described as a 'head-in-the-sand' solution to the problem.

He spotted some pine floorboards on a local skip and fixed them to the damp wall so that he was spared the sight of the spreading damp. On completion, he found the joins between the boards unsightly and the flat monotony uninspiring, and enlivened them with hand-carved fretwork cut from discarded pine doors. He continued carving for the next 19 years, cutting fretwork with intricate, layered patterns of abstract motifs and figurative detail for walls, ceilings and doors. He created for himself both a much-loved home and an entirely personal work of art which stands as a testament to his creative prowess.

Khadambi had no formal training in carving and was entirely self-taught. He did not commit his designs to paper, preferring to work out the design in his head and translate it directly to the wood. In this way, he devised the design of individual motifs, complete wall faces and entire rooms, demonstrating great visual acuity and ensuring the house stood as a coherent whole. He drew directly on to the wood and adapted his design as necessary as he responded to the wood itself. Although there are a number of different hacksaws and fretsaws in the house, Khadambi favoured a pad saw (a plasterboard blade in a Stanley knife housing). He used a drill to provide an entry point for the pad saw and then carved out the pattern or figure, leaving the edges with a rough unsanded finish.

The majority of the wood is seasoned pine from panelled doors and floorboards. On occasion, he did use new wood, for instance in the hallway, when the design demanded longer lengths. Once the steady flow of discarded wood in skips dried up, he carved from wine crates. He also incorporated a small amount of pre-carved wooden elements and parts of reclaimed furniture into his decorative schemes.

A significant amount of the fretwork was made while he was still in full-time employment in the civil service. He would work on the house in concentrated bursts, working fourteen-hour days for four to six days at a stretch. The carving was physically demanding and often laborious, but he remained rigorous and if he felt that a piece of carving was not right, he would consign it to the fire in the Sitting Room and start again. The fretwork is pinned and glued to surfaces, and pencil marks, blobs of glue and pins which aren't hammered home are readily discernible. This was not sloppiness on his part, but personal preference. He was unconcerned if evidence of his working methods survived, and was happy with the end result of each length of fretwork.

"I never copy … I look for inspiration and then change what I see to suit the space I have and the effect I want."
Khadambi Asalache

In 1995, when he had completed the Dining Room and Sitting Room, Khadambi gave a lecture on his work at the house to architecture students at the University of North London (now part of London Metropolitan University). He identified three distinct cultures which had left a "lasting impression" on him and which inspired his fretwork. These were: traditional African houses, Moorish architecture in Andalucia, and Ottoman architecture. In each case, he assimilated details from their distinct architectural vocabularies and subtly reworked them into his designs.

African houses

Khadambi was widely read and well travelled and drew on first-hand experience of the landscape of his childhood in western Kenya, buildings in Mombasa and Zanzibar, knowledge of the architecture of the Dogon tribe in Mali, and the 18th-century coral houses in Lamu, an island off the Kenyan coast.

Moorish architecture in Andalucia, Spain

Khadambi was moved by the architecture of Granada and Cordoba and recorded, "I have never failed to marvel at the Alhambra [in Granada] and even more impressive, the [Great] Mosque at Cordoba." The Alhambra is a complex of buildings akin to a fortified town, which includes gardens and a palace, and is celebrated as Spain's most significant example of Berber Islamic architecture. It was started in the mid-9th century and significantly added to by its Catholic rulers in the 16th century. The Great Mosque (La Mezquita) was begun *c.*785/6 and extended over ensuing centuries, before being radically altered by the erection of side-chapels and a cathedral, after Cordoba fell to the Christians in 1236.

Ottoman architecture

Khadambi was particularly drawn to the predominantly wooden, waterside mansions known as *Yali* which line the shores of the Bosphorus in Istanbul. The houses range in date from the late 17th to early 19th century and are often sophisticated architectural structures, with rich and elaborate wooden carvings to the main elevations overlooking the Bosphorus.

Because he found elements of African design static and self-contained and some Arabic designs to be elegant but repetitive, he "looked to Morocco and India" for motifs to provide linkage and a coherent flow from one element of his fretwork design to another. While there is no narrative to the fretwork, it is born of Khadambi's experience and enthusiasms and contains allusions to past memories and glimpses of architectural motifs which caught his imagination. The house is a synthesis of the many cultures he absorbed and gently filtered and reworked with his artist's eye.

"The knowledge that there is no symmetry in nature, made me think of harmony, not in terms of symmetry, but in terms of visual balance."
Khadambi Asalache

There is a purposeful lack of symmetry in the design and execution of the fretwork. Khadambi sought to achieve "a feeling of lightness and happiness" within the house through visual balance rather than by repetitive designs which resulted in a symmetrical whole. Although the lines and layers of pattern create a unified effect, each detail or motif is subtly different. He wanted the eye to move and catch the subtle variations in every run of carving.

The Great Mosque
at Cordoba

Tour of the House

Detail of fretwork in
the Dining Room

The Dining Room

This room contains the first fretwork carved by Khadambi Asalache. The west wall, opposite the fireplace, had a damp problem caused by the adjoining building, which was in use as a commercial laundry in the early 1980s. After covering the damp patch with floorboards fixed to the wall, he was unhappy with the appearance of the blank wood with its strong vertical lines and so embellished it with fretwork to enliven it and introduce movement and interest to the room. Once this first carving, which includes applied fretwork and slender shelves and niches built out from the wall, was completed, Khadambi recognised that the rest of the room would need to be treated in a similar way to ensure that the whole felt balanced and harmonious. Several years after he had carved the niches on the west wall, he discovered a tradition of strikingly similar niches, known as *zidaka*, on the island of Lamu, off the Kenyan coast. This led to a growing interest in the architecture of Lamu. In both instances, the niches were created as things of beauty in their own right and to hold prized possessions.

The fretwork is carefully wrought and characterised by variations in the number of layers. In some instances, there is a dense layering of pattern; in others, such as the framework around the Balinese goddess, who represents the triumph of good over evil, it is a simple detail. A fire surround has been constructed around the original range, and a half-screen shields one window from the street. Figures cut to resemble silhouettes huddle beneath palm trees, and flamingos are silhouetted against the foot of the hearth. A frieze of figures going to market, which resembles the carvings of the Makonde tribe in Mozambique, sits on a shelf opposite the windows. The room is furnished with functional, but intrinsically attractive, everyday objects – everything is carefully placed, and similar objects are grouped together for maximum visual impact. A collection of hot plates is suspended above the range, and the dresser displays glassware and oriental plates framed by fretwork against a collage of Botticelli's *Primavera*, which is pasted to the wall.

The Dining Room was the scene of many happy dinner parties presided over by Khadambi. Friends from the Treasury recall invitations to long lunches, when they would hop on the bus with Khadambi and arrive at his house to discover a delicious lunch of lamb curry in a slow cooker awaiting their arrival. His convivial dinner parties were planned weeks in advance to ensure he could get the necessary ingredients. Dried tuna flown in from Mombasa and then marinated in spices for several days was a particular favourite. He served his food without cutlery, in the knowledge that part of the pleasure of the food was the sensation of eating with fingers and chapattis. After dinner, his guests would be invited to see the house and to continue conversations by the fire in the Sitting Room. They would be seated on the low sofa, Asante stools or kilim cushions (tapestry-woven items produced in the area from the Balkans to Persia) on the floor, as the light from the fire and flickering candles cast shadows across the fretwork.

The range in the Dining Room
with heated plates suspended
from the mantelpiece

The Sitting Room

When Khadambi began work on the Sitting Room, the realisation of the enormity of the task ahead led him to employ a carpenter to translate his designs into physical form. It was a brief relationship which produced a short run of fretwork (less than a foot long) which Khadambi found to be competent but ultimately unsatisfactory. From this point onwards he undertook all of the design and execution himself.

This double reception room is lit by sash-windows to the north and south. In 1981, when Khadambi moved in, it still had both firegrates and one chimneypiece but the double doors had been removed from the central opening. Khadambi encased the 19th-century chimneypiece in the front Sitting Room in fretwork (leaving the original roundels exposed) and made shelves for the recesses to either side of the fireplaces.

The fretwork may be a single depth of wood or many-layered – creating a dramatic three-dimensional effect which adds depth and movement to the overall design. This is particularly well demonstrated by the fretwork niches which spring from the upper level of the wall and radiate onto the ceiling. Khadambi purposefully didn't square details off because he disliked sharp corners. He felt they stopped the eye dead, whereas he wanted the eye to move gently from the horizontal or vertical line of pattern to the adjoining plane.

The frieze of fretwork ballerinas above the mantelpiece in the Sitting Room caught in Act III of *Swan Lake* illustrates one such incident. Juxtaposed alongside the dancers are two gliding swans. Carved elephants stride across the top of the doorframe. An angel raises a trumpet in an exquisitely intricate panel to the right of the window to the street, and paired masks are carved into the window frame.

The mantelpiece in the
Sitting Room

The Rear Sitting Room

The shelves to the left and right of the fireplace house an attractive collection of pink lustreware porcelain. Khadambi originally designed them to stand alone as beautifully wrought shelves without the need for objects to draw the eye and embellish them. He calculated the space between each shelf on the basis of the Golden Ratio – a sequence of numbers derived from nature, where each successive number is the sum of the two previous numbers, for instance, 1, 1, 2, 3, 5, 8, 13 and so on. He recorded that "in arranging bookshelves the space between them is usually determined by how easy it is to put in and take out a book. In a display unit how well the article is displayed takes precedence over the units. But supposing you want to display shelving on its own? … Because of the way I have spaced the shelf units, and the design elements I have incorporated, there is no overriding need to put anything on them – the pink and copper lustre do not add anything to the design."

His approach to the fretwork and to all the other designed elements of his home was intellectually rigorous and aesthetically ruthless – if fretwork failed to meet his personal standard, it was burnt, and if a detail or object jarred, it was removed.

This is the first room in which Khadambi introduced painted detail to his design. He designed geometric forms which run across the middle of the room and around the edges of the kilim rugs to create an additional painted border and mixed linoleum paints to achieve the deep palette of colour. The fire surround was re-cast in bold colours as a continuation in painted form of the surface patterning, and the door to the Hall (which was always kept open and thus visible as part of the wider room) is painted with flowers and ducks on a pool of water which is delineated by a knot in the pine.

The play of light has a critical role throughout the house, and in the sitting rooms in particular. It is carefully orchestrated to accentuate natural light, to cast shadows and to subtly highlight details. There is painted decoration which takes the form of a shadow to the right of the window to the road. The pierced Moroccan shade to the pendant light throws a pattern of shadows onto the ceiling and onto the silver Ethiopian Coptic crosses on the mantelpiece. The fretwork lampshade to the standard lamp diffuses light over the copper dishes on the side-tables. In the evening, this room was always lit by candlelight and by the roaring wood fire, which was fed by a steady flow of off-cuts and lengths of carving which were deemed unsatisfactory.

In an extension in three-dimensional form to his decorative schemes, Khadambi made fretwork furniture or adapted existing pieces of furniture to serve a new purpose. The many-sided table was made to display his much-loved collection of pressed and moulded glass and silver inkwells. It is surrounded by slender miniature stools which serve a purely visual function.

The rich texture of the surface decoration is complemented by the naturalness with which disparate objects – postcards, bracelets, neck rests, Senegalese hangings, kilim cushions, Asante stools, books, glasses, icons, classical plaques and antique engravings – are arranged in intricate compositions. The unusual sits cheek-by-jowl with the everyday, but each carefully chosen and placed object has its own intrinsic beauty and contributes to the overall character of the room. Many of these objects were collected on holidays in Istanbul, Morocco and Tanzania or discovered in local junk shops or at antique fairs. Much of the early 19th-century pink and copper lustreware was purchased from markets in Greenwich, Covent Garden and Brighton. Khadambi's highly prized collection of inkwells was amassed over many years and rebuilt after a number were stolen. Other pieces were given by close friends and in one instance, a china plate was left on his doorstep with an anonymous note after someone had read about the house in a magazine article.

"I don't know or believe one needs to bother with concepts from quantum mechanics when doing interior design, but one can try."
Khadambi Asalache

The Rear Sitting Room
with the garden beyond

The Hall

The long planks of wood required for the near-horizontal lines which run the length of the Hall are one of the few instances in the house where Khadambi chose to use new, unseasoned timber. He purchased the wood in small quantities from the local builders' merchant Travis Perkins and carved, pinned and glued each length to the wall as quickly as possible to prevent it warping before returning to procure more wood. The staff at Travis Perkins were intrigued and hugely impressed when shown a photograph of the fretwork and presented him with a trade card.

By the back door, three antique prints of African scenes are framed by the fretwork and appear as though the fretwork has organically enveloped them into its design.

The fretwork patterns on the inner face of the front door embody Khadambi's deeply held belief that harmony can be achieved through visual balance. The two guardian angels positioned to "accompany home guests" after parties are complementary but not mirror images of one another.

The staircase with a reflected view of pink lustreware in the Rear Sitting Room

The Staircase and Landing

A rich array of fretwork rises up the walls of the
Staircase and Landing and fluently extends on to the
ceiling. This creates an extraordinarily beautiful and
contained space with a long vista framed by the window
with a view of the green of the garden beyond.

The Staircase is carpeted with a re-weave of the original
kilim runner which was cut from a larger rug to ensure the
perfect width was achieved. On the bottom step of the
Staircase it covers a large gash which resulted from the
removal of a 1930s "monstrosity of a fireplace" from the
Bedroom. As Khadambi was manoeuvring the fireplace,
he lost control of it and it crashed to the foot of the stair.

After Khadambi's death in 2006, the house suffered
from major subsidence and although this is now stabilised,
the scars of this structural movement are visible around
the stair window, which has dropped and forced the
fretwork to splinter away from the wall.

At the top of the Staircase, the skirting is decorated
with a minutely painted scene of Thomson Gazelles.
This was painted by Khadambi for the edification of his
partner's Tibetan Spaniel so that she had something to
delight her eye as she climbed the stair to the dog kennel
he constructed for her in the Bedroom.

The first-floor Landing;
the view shows the
Mimosa tree framed by
the window

The Bedroom

The Bedroom fretwork has a gently different character to that found in the Dining Room and Sitting Room. Elements of the fretwork more explicitly acknowledge the influence of Moorish Spain and the horseshoe arches of the Great Mosque at Cordoba in particular. The slender gracefulness of the fretwork on the walls and ceiling is accentuated by the floating wardrobes which Khadambi remodelled and set above the ground to enhance the sense of space.

The fretwork bedhead with carved male and female African deities was prompted by an exhibition on Africa held at the Royal Academy in London in 1995.

The window to the right has a carved screen which incorporates the initials 'S' and 'K', the first letters of his and his partner's names. Khadambi memorably recorded that he was "antipathetic to net curtains" and created the screen as an elegant, wooden variant.

The walls are painted freehand, and pencil lines of outline sketches are still visible; one of the horses, for instance, has a fifth leg drawn in pencil. Several of the designs (the grape and vine being one) are recognisable as stencil patterns from the 1980s which Khadambi was given by an interior designer friend whose work he admired. He chose not to employ them as stencils and adapted the designs and integrated them with his own imaginative painting to create his desired effect.

The evocative falling figure painted to the left of the bed in shadowy tones was added as a compliment to an illustrator friend before one of his visits to the house.

The Bedroom is rich in textiles – from the bedspread to the 1930s silk curtains and the layers of rugs on the floor. The rugs knit together like pieces of different jigsaws across the floor; the deep colours and fluent patterns of the kilims contrast with the striking knotted fringe of a Casa Pupo rug and goat skins.

The best place from which to view the ceiling decoration is from the window side of the bed. Khadambi designed the fretwork to appear to its best advantage when viewed from his pillow.

The Bedroom from the door

The Spare Bedroom

This room was used by Khadambi as his study. The top of the diminutive desk and the idiosyncratic chest of drawers were once part of the same piece of furniture before being refashioned in their present form.

The fretwork on the walls serves in part as a frame for the painted scenes on each of the four walls. Five of the seven paintings make direct reference to Africa. Khadambi was a considered and inquisitive traveller but did not like to take photographs of the places he visited (or to have his own photograph taken). He preferred to look and to hold memories of the colours, smells and scenes he experienced in his head. The painting above the fireplace depicts several recollected moments from a holiday in Zanzibar. His guide took him beyond the traditional tourist trail to a village where he met young girls in their white communion dresses. He also saw the protected species of monkey which initially scavenged charcoal and over generations evolved to need it as part of its diet.

The painting over the bed shows the journey of the River Nile from its source, through Dinka country (the blue figures are members of the Dinka tribe from southern Sudan who live in the Nile basin) and Omdurman (the largest Sudanese city on the western bank of the Nile, opposite Khartoum) to Alexandria.

On the north wall is a scene of animals roaming the East African bush, which may recall a childhood memory of Kenya. Beneath this a circular painting shows a young man tending goats. This may be a self-portrait: a glimpse of an earlier age in another country, when Khadambi whiled away the hours reading Shakespeare while looking after his family's goats.

The window gives a view of the expanse of the garden and a glimpse of the fretwork frame carved for climbing plants.

Wall painting of Zanzibar

The Bathroom and Kitchen

The Bathroom is a beautifully conceived space which is best appreciated with the door shut so that the run of fretwork which covers both wall and door is unbroken. A glimpse of Khadambi's character and eclectic taste is gained from the female heroines he chose to portray – Pocahontas, Sappho, Bessie Smith, Madame de Pompadour and Anna Pavlova – respectively a Virginian Indian, a poetess, a jazz singer, an arbiter of taste, and a prima ballerina.

In the Kitchen, Khadambi prepared delicious meals for his many friends and for dinner parties of 12. All of the foodstuffs found in the cupboards were his and hint at the wonderful food he served in tagines and cooking pots taken straight from the oven to the table in the adjoining Dining Room.

Left Detail of hand-painted decoration and fretwork around the bathroom window

Below The Kitchen dresser

The Garden

The Garden faces south-east and is 5.5m wide by 19m long. In 1981 the garden was steeply sloping and contained several tumbledown sheds. It had most recently housed animals rather than plants. Khadambi was drawn to the garden because it was quiet (the house cuts out the noise from road traffic), was often sunny and was little overlooked, as there were only two properties to either side with an indirect view. To the rear of the end boundary fence is the garden of 577 Wandsworth Road, which extends in an L-shape, and beyond this is the former graveyard to St Paul's Church (built in 1815 on the site of the former parish church to the village of Clapham). In 2000 the section of the graveyard immediately behind the house was turned into the Eden Community Garden.

Khadambi began by terracing the garden onto three levels and stocking it with his favourite plants including roses, ferns and delphiniums. He planted a mimosa tree (a member of the Acacia family and a native of East Africa) outside the Rear Sitting Room window. The garden had a strong structure and he chose plants carefully for their leaf shape, flower, colour and texture. Fretwork structures were built out from the fences on both sides of the garden, creating a climbing frame for plants and shade for seating. A brick path runs half the length of the garden past the door to the disused privy and the early street lamp erected by Khadambi.

Khadambi carved all the fretwork for the house and garden outside on the bridge over the 'Crocodile Pit', the concrete path from the back of the house to the garden. He worked in all weathers, supporting the timber on his knee or on bricks.

The mimosa tree flourished and came to dominate the north-east end of the garden. It also dominated the view out into the garden from the Rear Sitting Room and the Spare Bedroom where its sculptural form and large, frond-like leaves drew the eye. Khadambi would climb the tree periodically and lop off a branch growing too close to the house. Unfortunately, the mimosa had to be cut down in 2011, because its roots had grown so large that they were threatening the stability of the house.

Rear elevation from the garden, including the mimosa tree planted by Khadambi

Khadambi Asalache

Born in Kapsabet near Kaimosi in western Kenya in 1935, Khadambi was the eldest son of a local chief and is said to have exhibited his literary bent as a child by herding cattle while reading Shakespeare. He was educated at a Catholic High School and read architecture at the Royal Technical College in Nairobi before leaving to travel to Europe to study fine art in Rome, Geneva and Vienna. In 1960, he moved to London and made it his home. He spent the 1960s and early 1970s concentrating on his literary career, publishing a critically acclaimed novel, *A Calabash of Life*, in 1967 and writing poetry which was broadcast on Radio 3 and appeared in the *Times Literary Supplement, Prism*, the *Transatlantic Review* and other periodicals and anthologies. In 1971, his second novel, *The Latecomer*, was broadcast on the BBC Africa Service and in 1973, his volume of poetry, *Sunset in Naivasha*, was published. His first novel became an exam text in a number of African countries and his work is widely respected and recognised to be influential. *The Companion to African Literature* (published in 2000) notes that "he has a place among the pioneers of modern Kenyan literature in English."

In the mid-1970s he joined the Civil Service, working first in the Civil Service Department and later in the Treasury and Cabinet Office, where he is said to have amazed one Treasury Mandarin by writing his notes in blank verse. He gained an MPhil with distinction in the Philosophy of Mathematics in the 1970s and went on to combine this knowledge with his architectural training in the design of the interiors at Wandsworth Road. He began carving fretwork in 1986 and worked on the decoration and furnishing of his house for 19 years. In 2005, he declared the house to be finished.

Throughout this time, he entertained many friends and acquaintances and was a generous and charismatic host. He was also a talented, instinctive cook who derived great pleasure from others' delight in his food, conversation and home.

Khadambi Asalache
in London

"This house reflects a deep-rooted belief in the link between effort and attainment. The influence of Khadambi's early years in Kenya, living in London – a place he loved, the sense of returning home [to Kenya] only as an outsider, and his keen appreciation of the multiplicity of traditions left a legacy which bridges perceptions. Within the expression of his creativity he allows us into his own world."
Susie Thomson, 2006

"Khadambi Asalache hid his many talents under a gentle personality. He was a private man, an idealistic aesthete who had learnt to view life with amusement."
The Times obituary by Ann Barr (former editor of *Tatler* and editor of *The Sloane Ranger's Handbook*), 2006

Conserving the House

The house has suffered from rising damp, subsidence, a leaking roof and severe cracking to the original, early 19th-century lath-and-plaster ceilings. From 2011 to 2013 the National Trust undertook a major conservation project to stabilise the ceilings, all of which are embellished with fretwork; contain the damp in the Dining Room; make the house watertight; renew all services; and introduce a fire-suppression system.

The guiding principle of the project was that all problems should be addressed in the knowledge of Khadambi Asalache's own pragmatic and creative approach.

One of the most critical elements was tackling the plaster ceilings which were in imminent danger of collapse due to the failure of the plaster to adhere to the structural supports. This cracking was caused by a number of factors including the decay of the plaster over time, poor craftsmanship, a history of water ingress in the attic space, vibration caused by the footfall of visitors to the house following Khadambi's death and subsidence to the rear elevation. Another element was the problem of damp, which rose from the ground to a height of 1.8 metres in the Dining Room even though the adjoining building was no longer in use as a commercial laundry.

Just as Khadambi had done, we had to accept the ongoing presence of damp and find a solution which did not cause the lime plaster to crumble or the panelling and fretwork to rot over time. A dry lining membrane was introduced which allows the rising damp to circulate across the wall surface and escape through an air gap. The nature of the intricate fretwork surfaces, hand-painted floors and small scale of the rooms means that the house remains a fragile place and for this reason we limit the number of visitors each year.

Conserving the fragile fretwork
on the Bedroom ceiling